S.T.E.M.

Genesis Griffin

Presentation by *BookLeaf Publishing*

Web: www.bookleafpub.com

E-mail: info@bookleafpub.com

ISBN: 9789357740128

First edition 2023

To Sarah, Veve, and Juicy,

Psalms 91

ACKNOWLEDGEMENT

To Abba,

Thank you for always being there for me.

PREFACE

This book of poems was written to give hope to the newly aged adults who feel lost and are just roaming the Earth in search of their purpose.

I am now choosing to follow my dreams of becoming an author. All my life, I've been living in the shadow of others' perceptions of me, and now, 22 years later, I have decided to take control of my life.

Exist, Heal, and Live for YOU.

The Sensory Cortex

Can you hear me?

I am crying out for help.

Why don't you see me?

I must be sporting an invisible cloak.

Can you hear me?

I am begging you to listen.

Why don't you see me?

Eyes blurred; vision shot.

Can you hear me?

You chose not to listen.

Why don't you see me?

I'm Timmy Turner.

Scared;

To journey this alone,

but you've given me no choice…

Substance P

3

Spinning out of control
and I can't stop.
Pain radiating in my temporal lobes
and it won't stop.
Stress has become overwhelming
and it is beyond me.
Nociceptors are firing;
temporal pain has become somatic pain.
Bills sky-high,
covering the horizon.

Abba, take me away,

          away,

              away,

to where my dreams last forever…

Critical Condition

Sensory Neurons:
When you stare in the mirror,
Who is staring back at you?

Interneurons:
- Fear
- Doubt
- Shame
- Detachment

Motor Neurons:
DANGER!
DANGER!
DANGER!

The patient is in critical condition…

Diagnosis: Self-abandonment.

Prescription: Who are you?

Genetics

5

We DO NOT pick our parents,

We DO NOT pick our shortcomings,

We DO NOT pick our brains, hair, body, eyes,
feet, hands, nails, and

We DO NOT pick our thoughts, fears, or doubts.

We were CHOSEN but,

We all have a STORY.

Whether XX, XXY, XY, and anything in
between
we are more
than
our
genetics.

RISE

Homeostasis

The human body was designed like a
house.
Everything that we need to survive
is placed under our skin.

The human body was designed like a
house.
My favorite gland acquires our body's
functionality;
The hypothalamus.

On and off like a light switch,
the hypothalamus understands
our needs.
On and off like a light switch,
homeostasis is carried out.

Unfortunately, our thoughts don't
come with a built-in
thermostat that tells us
when to
shut up and drive.

However,
conduct that experiment

and become a
controlled variable
that is
consistent and
unwavering.

Opinions

Some microorganisms can be harmful to you
and others not so much but either way
must wash your hands.

Metamorphosis

Our seeds go through many transformations.
Just like everything in this world,
Our seeds go through the cycle of life.

As we change
mentally,
physically,
emotionally,
so do our seeds.

We grow, but…

We tend to forget that
our seeds are what we need.
We tend to forget that
our seeds are undeveloped flowers.
We tend to forget that
our flowers are meant to be seen.

How to remember?

Keep germinating.

Action Potential

Nothing in the body works until
an action potential is reached.

…to be in a constant state of immobility.
Never being able to move the limbs.

Imagine never reaching full potential…

Leaving room for imagination…

…to be in a constant state of regret.
Never being able to grasp what could've
been.

What is holding back your rising phase?

Failure?

It's okay to overshoot and fall. Hard. Trust the
process. You'll start again.

Viral

Our bodies are strong enough to withstand any
pathogenic attack but,
sometimes we must seek medical attention.
That virus can be lethal.

Untreated, we can fall under many influences.

As much as we try to avoid these infectious
diseases,
We come into contact with them every day
through
the daily interactions with others.

Untreated, we can fall under many influences.

Of course, we can fight them ourselves
but there are times when help is needed.

We aren't meant to deal with these issues
by our lonesome.

Emotionally is where it hits us the most....

It's okay to ask for help.

The Holy Trinity

Red Blood Cells,
White Blood Cells,
and
Platelets.

These elements are our lifesavers.
You can try and live without them, but
hematology begs a differ.
Without these elements within us,
we are sacks of dried, infected organs.

Erythrocytes,
Leukocytes,
and
Thrombocytes.

Elements of our circulatory system.
Necessary for survival;
the functionality of the mind, body, and soul.

Oxygen,
Immunity,
and
Clotting.

In togetherness, we are whole.

Heart vs. Soul

Heart: Our strongest memories lie here.

Soul: All that we are resigns here.

Good or bad,

the heart pumps;

only for survival.

We prod our thoracic cavity,

looking for what is digestible for others,

however, we wish to show the truth.

But the soul…

it won't yield.

The soul will shine…

only if you let it.

Lysosomes are cool.

Lysosomes are cool.
Why?
They get rid of waste, toxins, and other products
that the body's cell doesn't need.

Lysosomes are cool.
Why?
They remind me of the importance of boundaries
and
personal growth.

Lysosomes are cool.
Why?
It keeps the body healthy and protects it against
infection.

Lysosomes are cool.
Why?
They remind me that it is important to get rid of
anything
that can stop me from striving.

Lysosomes are cool.
Why?
Builds up the cell's protective membrane.

Lysosomes are cool.
Why?
They remind me that sometimes life can break
me down
but Abba is always there to build me back up.

You the Parasite

17

Sometimes it's not even other people...

The type of relationship you have with yourself matters, too.

Cortisol and the Silent Killer

Be aware!
It attacks the mind first and next the body.

…cortisol up.

Be ready to fight back!
Regulate what you can control and then rest.

…cortisol down.

Be aware!
It comes like a thief in the night and steals all life.

…cortisol up.

Be ready to fight back!
Regulate your focus and your peace.

…cortisol down.

SAVE YOURSELVES BEFORE IT'S TOO LATE!!!

Guard your Gates

Bacteria rule the world.
Just like microbes, opinions are invisibly
infectious.
Not all are harmful but others…
To coexist would be like existing during that
Chlorea Epidemic.

I say all that to say this,
Leukopenia is a real thing.
The body cannot fight off antigens without its
leukocytes.
Low White Blood Cell count can lead to fatality.

Think of others' perception of you as bacteria,
while it is okay to adhere to some, like E.Coli in
the gut,
others can get you down.
Think of leukopenia as the lack of protection
over your journey;
at that point, your future is at stake.
I'd say guard your gates.

Photosynthesis

Plants never worry.
Through photosynthesis,
all they need is sunlight, enough water, and
some CO2.
Seasonally, they grow and die, yet don't worry.

If I were a plant,
I'd be a worry plant.
My receptors would synthesize doubt, lots of
shame, and tons of anxiety.
I'd grow,
wither,
shrivel.

Sometimes it is hard…
it is hard to believe that all we must do is be
present
and that everything we need will be provided for
us naturally.

Like plants, all we must do is be present to soak
it all up.

Got Mitochondria?

21

Life can suck all the energy from you.
Feelings of Lethargy.
There is no avoiding it.

However, the truth is we have a choice.
Freedom or bondage.
You have to choose.

Rest up.
Gather your strength.
Palms upwards towards the sun.

…hitchhiking SAD is only passing through.

Mutualism

Bacteria live everywhere and on everything,
even in the human body.
Escherichia coli,
Bacteroides thetaiotaomicron, and
Staphylococcus epidermidis.

The human body was designed based on the
concept
of being in community with one another.
Abba,
Family, and
Friends.

The idea of mutualistic relationships is that both
parties benefit from each other.
Relationships,
Mentorship, and
Fellowship.

Just like the human body cannot thrive without
its own
unique set of bacteria, we cannot strive in
isolation.

Osteogenesis

Up to a certain age, our bones are broken and rebuilt.

For us to become better people, we grow.

Growing and changing boys hit puberty, and that growth spurt happens.

Life is meant to bring us growing pains, and we are strong.

Osteoclasts break down the old bone, and osteoblasts remodel and rebuild.

We aren't designed to remain the same even if we try to be.

Parasympathetic

It's time for rest.
It's time for release.
It's time for relaxation.

Forget the troubles.
Forget the worries.
Forget the doubts.

I am done looking over my shoulder.
I am done looking for an escape.
I am done looking for safety in the dark.

Peace is near.
Joy is present.
Faith is here.

REM

dREaM big.
dREaM loud.

There is nothing in this world that is
untouchable.

Make all that you "be" come true.
It's never too late to close your eyes
and believe in what is not there YET.

Imagine. Cultivate. REM